ISRAEL
Photography & Decrees

by
Faytene C. Grasseschi

© Copyright April 2013

Israel Photography & Decrees By Faytene C. Grasseschi

Large Print Edition

Unless otherwise referenced all Scripture quotations are taken from the NEW INTERNATIONAL VERSION®. Scripture quoted by permission. Quotations designated (NIV) are from THE HOLY BIBLE: NEW INTERNATIONAL VERSION®. NIV®. Copyright © 1973, 1978, 1984 by Biblica. All rights reserved worldwide.

Photography & graphic design by Faytene C. Grasseschi.

Self published by Faytene C. Grasseschi. Printed by Lightening Source.

ISBN: 978-0-9891017-0-7

"And the Almighty will be thy treasure, And precious silver unto thee. For then shalt thou delight thyself in the Almighty, And shalt lift up thy face unto God. Thou shalt make thy prayer unto him, and he will hear thee; And thou shalt pay thy vows. **Thou shalt also decree a thing, and it shall be established unto thee**; And light shall shine upon thy ways. When they cast [thee] down, thou shalt say, [There is] lifting up; And the humble person he will save."

(Job 22: 25-29, American Standard Version)

Special Thanks To:

Holy Spirit. Thank You for empowering us to bring glory to Jesus.

Rebekah Larzelere, Simone Alex, Krista MacLeod, Sarah Johnson, Jo Jo Smith, Barb Shakall-Barkey & Ruth Stephens for your editing help & encouragement in the writing process.

My amazing husband Robert John. You are such a gift. Thank you for your ongoing love & support.

All our amazing family, friends & partners. We love you so much.
Thank you for supporting & standing with us in the call.

ISRAEL
BOOK OF
PHOTOGRAPHY & DECREES

TABLE OF CONTENTS

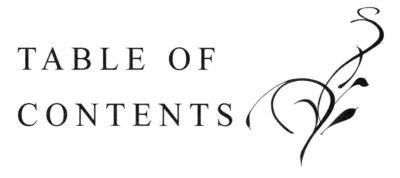

Preface

11 - Day One: The Garden of Gethsemane / Consecration

15 - Day Two: The Eastern Wall & Gate / God's Rule

19 - Day Three: Galgotha: The Place of the Skull / Blood of Jesus

23 - Day Four: The Garden Tomb / Resurrection Power

27 - Day Five: The Upper Room / Holy Spirit

31 - Day Six: The Western Wall / Spirit of Prayer

35 - Day Seven: Temple Stones / Truth

39 - Day Eight: Temple Mount / Trust

43 - Day Nine: Christian Quarter / Spirit of Adoption

47 - Day Ten: Church of the Holy Sepulcher / Faith

51 - Day Eleven: Arab Children / Childlike Hearts & Harvest

55 - Day Twelve: The Arab Quarter / Harvest

59 - Day Thirteen : Jewish Children / God's Faithfulness

63 - Day Fourteen: Elderly Jewish Men / Longevity & Honor

67 - Day Fifteen: Jewish Families & Children / Inheritance & Aliyah

71 - Day Sixteen: City of David / Authority

75 - Day Seventeen: Jewish Tombs / Eternal Mindset

79 - Day Eighteen: Israeli Defense Force / Protection

83 - Day Nineteen: The Security Wall / Reconciliation

87 - Day Twenty: The Dead Sea / Salt of the Earth

91 - Day Twenty - One: Masada / Perseverance & Determination

95 - Day Twenty - Two: Desert Cave / Hidden Treasures

99 - Day Twenty - Three: The Bedouins / God's Voice

103 - Day Twenty - Four: Capernaum / Signs & Wonders

107 - Day Twenty - Five: The Galilee / God's Light

111 - Day Twenty - Six: Mount of Beatitudes / Character

115 - Day Twenty - Seven: Gideon's Brook / Trust In God's Strength

119 - Day Twenty - Eight: Joppa / Mercy

123 - Day Twenty - Nine: Caesarea / Advancement of the Gospel

127 - Day Thirty: Megiddo / Discernment & Awakening

131 - Day Thirty - One: Tel Aviv / Restoration

Preface

This book is dedicated to the lover of my soul, Jesus Christ. It is also dedicated to you, the reader.

I am so grateful to have had the opportunity to journey with Jesus to His homeland of Israel & to be able to share some of that journey with you through these pages. The photographs in this book were taken on a journey of love as I put my hand in His & discovered Israel over several ministry trips there. My heart in publishing this book of photography & was to share these images with you. This book is for anyone with a love for Israel (especially those who have not been able to visit it in person but have wanted to) & anyone who is simply wanting to go deeper in their relationship with God.

Secondly, over the years I have found that decreeing God's Word over my life has been totally transforming. His Word is true! If we decree a thing in alignment with His will, it will be established (Job 22:25-29). What we speak over our lives, our loved ones & various situations is so powerful. Because of this, I was compelled to accompany these photographs with declarative prayers (decrees).

The photographs & decrees are organized into 31 days - one for each day of the month. With each day you will encounter a new visual display of photographs from Israel, an accompanying scripture reading & declarative prayer that you can decree over your life & the lives of your loved ones.

Lastly, before we dive in I want to give the disclaimer that I pretty much have a "go big or go home" mentality in prayer. Because of this, many of the decrees encompass an aspect of praying regionally, nationally or globally as well. While praying for ourselves I figure we have nothing to lose in praying for the whole world as well. Our God is so big! I absolutely love honoring Him with big prayers.

I pray that you will enjoy taking in these visual moments, decrees & prayers as much as I enjoyed writing them. May our hearts continue to expand with deep love for Israel & may His richest blessings fall upon you today.

Thank you for joining me as we journey through these pages.

God bless you,

Faytene Grasseschi

Faytene Grasseschi

Day One
The Garden of Gethsemane

The Garden of Gethsemane

Scripture Reading:

"Then Jesus went with his disciples to a place called Gethsemane, and he said to them, "Sit here while I go over there and pray.'... Going a little farther, he fell with his face to the ground and prayed, "My Father, if it is possible, may this cup be taken from me. Yet not as I will, but as you will." (Matthew 26:36-39)

About These Photographs:

This is the Garden of Gethsemane where Jesus spent His final hours of prayer before being arrested, tried & then crucified on the Cross. It is carefully cared for today by gardeners like this wonderful man in the top photograph so that we can gaze on it & meditate on Jesus' prayer time there. The Garden of Gethsemane is at the base of the Mount of Olives & directly across from the Eastern Gate of the Old City of Jerusalem.

Decree / Prayer on the Theme of Consecration: *Jesus, thank You for embracing the will of the Father as You prayed in the Garden of Gethsemane. I honor You for Your unswerving willingness to do whatever He asked. I decree over my soul that I desire to do the will of the Father as well - no matter what the cost is. I pray in agreement with Your own words Jesus & declare, "Father not my will but Yours be done." Not only do I decree a spirit of consecration over my life, but I also ask for the wisdom to discern the will of the Father in every moment. I decree a spirit of prevailing prayer over my life just as You prevailed in prayer in this garden. Jesus, I thank You that as You prayed here You did not focus on the price but the prize. You saw the prize as greater than the sacrifice & determined to lay everything down to do the will of Your Father (Hebrews 12:12). I decree over my soul as well that I will live for eternal purposes & for the pleasure of God – nothing else. Thank You for pouring Your Holy Spirit upon me in a fresh way today so that I might be willing to crucify my will to the will of the Father. Be glorified in my life I pray in Jesus' name.*

Day Two

The Eastern Wall & Eastern Gate

The Eastern Gate

Scripture Reading:

"The LORD said to me, "This gate is to remain shut. It must not be opened; no one may enter through it. It is to remain shut because the LORD, the God of Israel, has entered through it...He is to enter by way of the portico of the gateway and go out the same way."
(Ezekiel 44:2-3)

About These Photographs:

This is the Eastern Wall & Eastern Gate of the Old City of Jerusalem. On the other side of the Eastern Wall is the Temple Mount where the First Temple & Second Temple once were. In front of the Eastern Wall is an Arab graveyard. The Eastern Gate has been sealed up so that nothing enters in or goes out of it. Many believe that according to Ezekiel 44:2-3, Jesus will enter through this gate when He returns to establish His ultimate rule in the earth. While Jesus was praying in the Garden of Gethsemane He would have been looking straight at this gate - perhaps visualizing the great day of His return.

Decree / Prayer For The Release Of The Rule of Christ In The Earth: *Jesus, I thank You that You came once & You are coming again. I honor You for Your kingship & rule. You have prevailed over death, hell & the grave & You will soon rule over the nations in Your second coming. Today, I decree an increased revelation into my heart regarding the reality of Your second coming & dominion. I decree Your kingship & total rule over my life & the lives of my loved ones. I decree that I live in light of Your return & the reality of eternity. Even as the graves in front of the Eastern Gate embody the spirit of death, I decree the spirit of life over my heart, mind, soul & the lives of my loved ones. I also decree life over the Arab community & Jewish community both in Israel & throughout the nations of the earth. I ask that You would release over them an increasing revelation of the reality of Your first & second coming. Jesus, would You also release a revelation of Your second coming to the nations of the earth. I decree this now in the name of Jesus & thank You for Your awesome Kingly power. You rule & will rule forever!*

Day Three

Galgotha
The Place of the Skull

Golgotha / The Hill of the Skull

Scripture Reading:

"Carrying his own cross, he went out to the place of the Skull (which in Aramaic is called Golgotha). Here they crucified him, and with him two others - one on each side and Jesus in the middle. Pilate had a notice prepared and fastened to the cross. It read: jesus of nazareth, the king of the jews." (John 19:17-19)

About These Photographs:

This is the hill where many believe Jesus was crucified. It is located just outside the Old City of Jerusalem in an Arab neighborhood. It is also a very short distance from what many people believe is the Garden Tomb. This hill is called the Hill of the Skull because it has a formation in it that resembles a skull. The formation has eroded over the years, but pictures dating back a few decades show the formation of the skull face much more clearly than what you can see today (see image in the bottom photograph).

Decree / Prayer To Apply The Power of The Blood of Jesus: *Jesus, I honor You for Your sacrifice on the Cross. I honor Your blood that was spilled for my sins & the sins of the whole world. Today, I decree a fresh revelation into my heart regarding the price You paid for my salvation & the power of Your redeeming blood. I plead Your blood over my life & the lives of my loved ones. I also declare that no weapon formed against us shall prosper. I also decree the revelation of Your powerful & saving blood over my loved ones who do not yet know You. Let this revelation come into their hearts & minds. I decree that every area of my life is under the redeeming power of Your blood & I thank You Jesus that because You died on the Cross, I am redeemed. I also pray for the inhabitants of Jerusalem, all of Israel & the ends of the earth. I pray for a revelation of Your blood to come upon them today in Jesus' name. Let Your salvation penetrate the hearts of unbelievers everywhere. I loose it now in Jesus' name.*

Day Four
The Garden Tomb

The Garden Tomb

Scripture Reading:

"At the place where Jesus was crucified, there was a garden, and in the garden a new tomb, in which no one had ever been laid." (John 19:41) "After the Sabbath, at dawn on the first day of the week, Mary Magdalene and the other Mary went to look at the tomb...The angel said to the women, 'Do not be afraid, for I know that you are looking for Jesus, who was crucified. He is not here; he has risen, just as he said. Come and see the place where he lay.'" (Matthew 28:1, 5-6)

About These Photographs:

These photos show the site believed by many to be the tomb where Jesus was placed after He was crucified. The tomb is in the side of a hill & has an area where a large stone can be rolled in front of the doorway to seal it shut. It meets the description of John 19 very well & is a very popular place of pilgrimage for believers visiting Jerusalem.

Decree / Prayer For Resurrection Power: *I decree Your resurrection power over my life & over the lives of my loved ones today. I receive by faith a fresh revelation of Your resurrection power even now. I speak over my body, soul, mind, finances, relationships & everything pertaining to my life & I call forth Your resurrection power! In every area of my life where the enemy has tried to bring death & decay I decree Your reviving strength. I call back seven times of what the enemy has stolen (Prov. 6:31). I thank You Jesus that You are more powerful than death. I thank You that You have also commissioned me to walk in that same resurrection power. I step into it by faith even now. I ask You to baptize me with Your resurrection power to such an extent that everywhere I go things come to life for Your glory. I also pray for Israel today. I call forth Your resurrection power to flow through the streets of Jerusalem, Israel & to the ends of the earth for Your name's sake. Thank You Jesus that You always do what You say. You said You would rise & You did (John 2:19)! I choose to stand firm in the victory of Your resurrection power.*

Day Five

The Upper Room

The Upper Room

Scripture Reading:

"When the day of Pentecost came, they were all together in one place. Suddenly a sound like the blowing of a violent wind came from heaven and filled the whole house where they were sitting. They saw what seemed to be tongues of fire that separated and came to rest on each of them. All of them were filled with the Holy Spirit and began to speak in other tongues as the Spirit enabled them.…Peter replied, 'Repent and be baptized, every one of you...'...Those who accepted his message were baptized, and about three thousand were added to their number that day."
(Acts 2:1-4, 38-41)

About These Photographs:

This is the Upper Room where 120 of Jesus' faithful followers gathered after His resurrection & tarried until the Holy Spirit fell with such power that thousands came to Christ through their preaching. Many believers, like the one in the top picture, still come here today to wait on God. The picture on the bottom left is of a curious on-looker peering into the room (an Orthodox Jewish man). He likely came from King David's Tomb right beneath the Upper Room. The architecture of the Upper Room is simple but stunning. Most stunning of all, however, is the lingering presence of Holy Spirit.

Decree / Prayer To Be Empowered By Holy Spirit: *Jesus, You said it was good for You to leave because if You did You would send the Holy Spirit to help us. Thank You for the precious gift of Holy Spirit. Holy Spirit, I love You & I ask that You would baptize me afresh today with Your power & fire in a way that I have not yet encountered. Empower me with Your gifts so I can glorify Jesus in greater measure through my life. I also decree a fresh baptism of the Holy Spirit & fire upon the entire church of Jesus Christ. I pray You would move powerfully in the streets of Jerusalem, in all of Israel & into the ends of the earth. Today, I decree a fresh empowerment upon us as believers to speak Your Word boldly just as the apostles did in Acts 2 when they saw thousands saved. Father, we thank You that You told us in Your Word that no one comes to You unless the Holy Spirit draws them. Draw people today, Holy Spirit. Even as You drew the Orthodox man in this photograph, I decree a drawing of multitudes to You today. I call forth & decree a fresh baptism of the Holy Spirit & fire in my life & into the ends of the earth. Come Holy Spirit!*

Day Six
The Western Wall

The Western Wall

Scripture Reading:

"As for the foreigner who does not belong to your people Israel but has come from a distant land because of your great name and your mighty hand and your outstretched arm-- when he comes and prays toward this temple, then hear from heaven, your dwelling place, and do whatever the foreigner asks of you, so that all the peoples of the earth may know your name and fear you, as do your own people Israel, and may know that this house I have built bears your Name." (2 Chronicles 6:32-33)

About These Photographs:

This is the Western Wall in Jerusalem which makes up one side of the Temple Mount. The Wall is one of the holiest sites in Judaism. The Jewish community gathers here to pray continuously. Many of those prayers are for the coming of the Messiah & the re-establishment of the Temple on the Temple Mount (where the Dome of the Rock currently is). The Wall is separated into two sections: the right side for women & the left side for men. In front of the designated prayer area is a large courtyard. Sometimes when you approach the Western Wall you will hear the men singing Psalms of David together. On Friday evenings (Shabbat) school children sing songs & dance traditional dances in the courtyard. This area is a place for prayer, reflection, repentance & also a place for joyous community celebration. You might think it would be a tense place given its proximity to the Dome of the Rock. To the contrary, it is generally very peaceful. God is there, listening to prayer, just as King Solomon asked Him to in 2 Chronicles 6.

Decree / Prayer For The Spirit of Prayer: *Father, I thank You that You are a God who hears & answers prayer. I call forth a fresh grace to pray into my life today. I also decree a fresh revelation of You into the hearts of every person who prays at this Western Wall. I ask that You would answer every prayer in alignment with Your will. Thank You for the hope in Your promises that this Wall represents. I decree a fresh spirit of hope & faith into my prayer life today, my loved ones' prayer lives & the lives of each person gathered at the Wall. You said that You would build a new temple made of living stones – which are Your people – & that You would dwell in our midst. With this in mind, I call forth a fresh release of Your presence dwelling in the midst of my life, my loved ones lives & Your people across the earth today. Thank You in advance for all these & more answered prayers.*

Day Seven

Temple Stones

Temple Stones

Scripture Reading:

"Some of his disciples were remarking about how the temple was adorned with beautiful stones and with gifts dedicated to God. But Jesus said, 'As for what you see here, the time will come when not one stone will be left on another; every one of them will be thrown down.'...He replied: "Watch out that you are not deceived. For many will come in my name, claiming, 'I am he,' and, 'The time is near.' Do not follow them..." (Luke 21:5-8)

About These Photographs:

This is a portion of the Western Wall of the Old City of Jerusalem. Archeologists say that some of these stones (the larger ones at the bottom) date back to the time of Jesus. Therefore, it is very possible that Jesus would have walked on the very stones in the top photograph. The stones in the Temple Wall are different sizes & configurations because of the various times that the Temple was rebuilt. Each type of stone is from a different phase in the building & re-building process.

Decree / Prayer For The Spirit Of Truth: *Jesus, thank You that You said Holy Spirit would lead & guide us into all truth. Holy Spirit, I acknowledge that You are the very Spirit of truth & council. I decree an open heaven over my heart, soul, mind & spirit to accurately receive & interpret truth from You. I call upon You for wisdom, discernment, revelation, & knowledge to be able to accurately discern the times I am living in, the steps I need to take & how to interact with those around me. I rebuke the spirit of deception. I come out of alignment with it's influence in any area of my life & I receive Your truth in all areas of my life in Jesus' name. If there is any area where I am not aligned with truth, I ask You to adjust it now in Jesus' name. I also decree this spirit of wisdom over my loved ones so that they might also discern & understand Your heart, Your will & Your ways. Thank You Lord that You said that if anyone lacks wisdom to just ask & that You would give it liberally (James 1:5). I receive a fresh outpouring of wisdom into my life today. I also pray for the leaders of Israel, my nation & the nations of the earth. I decree wisdom & understanding over them. Because You said the fear of the Lord is the beginning of wisdom, I call forth the fear of the Lord to powerfully impact them now in Jesus' name. Thank You for Your truth Lord.*

Day Eight

The Temple Mount

The Temple Mount

Scripture Reading:

"Some time later God tested Abraham. He said to him, 'Abraham!' 'Here I am,' he replied. Then God said, 'Take your son, your only son, Isaac, whom you love, and go to the region of Moriah. Sacrifice him there as a burnt offering on one of the mountains I will tell you about.' Early the next morning Abraham got up and saddled his donkey. He took with him two of his servants and his son Isaac. When he had cut enough wood for the burnt offering, he set out for the place God had told him about." (Genesis 22: 1-3)

About These Photographs:

This is the Temple Mount. It is the place where many Rabbis believe God gathered dust to create the first man, Adam. It is also believe to be the place where Abraham offered up Isaac, the location of the First & Second Temple & where many believe the Third Temple will be built in the future. It is the holiest site in Judaism, the 3rd holiest site of Sunni Muslims & one of the most contentious religious sites in the world. In the 1967 War, when Israel gained control of Jerusalem, as an act of peace the Israeli government gave control of the Temple Mount to the Arab community. Today the entire Temple Mount is a large courtyard with the main structure being the Dome of the Rock.

Decree / Prayer to Trust God Completely: *Lord, I declare that my trust is in You alone. I recognize, that like Abraham, I might not always understand Your ways in advance but I choose to trust You knowing that in the end You will come through. In all things, I recognize that Your ways are higher than mine (Isaiah 55:8). I repent for any way that I have not trusted You & as a result tried take control of my life in a wrong way. I decree a fresh spirit of faith over my heart, soul & mind to completely trust You in all things. I choose today to trust You with my past failings, my future path, my health, finances, family & all I hold dear. I place my whole life in Your hands because You are trustworthy. I also decree an increased grace to trust You & Your ways over all my loved ones. I thank You that they are increasing in surrender to You everyday. Finally Lord, I call forth this same level of trust to fill the hearts of the Jewish people, the Arab people & all the people of the earth! Let the revelation of Your faithfulness & trustworthiness fill the whole world in Jesus' name.*

Day Nine

The Christian Quarter

The Christian Quarter

Scripture Reading:

"While Jesus was still talking to the crowd, his mother and brothers stood outside, wanting to speak to him. Someone told him, 'Your mother and brothers are standing outside, wanting to speak to you.' He replied to him, 'Who is my mother, and who are my brothers?' Pointing to his disciples, he said, 'Here are my mother and my brothers. For whoever does the will of my Father in heaven is my brother and sister and mother."

(Matthew 12:46-50)

About These Photographs:

These are a few photographs from the very edge of the Old City of Jerusalem in & near the Christian Quarter. There are many amazing sites in the Christian Quarter including the Upper Room, the room where the Last Supper was, David's Tomb & more. The church building in the lower photographs is a stunning Catholic church in the heart of it all.

Decree / Prayer on for the Spirit of Adoption: Lord, I thank You that Your Word clearly says that any who call upon the name of Jesus will be saved & therefore adopted into Your family eternally (Romans 10:13). Jesus, I confess You as Lord & savior & thank You for making a way for me to be reconciled to my Heavenly Father through Your sacrifice on the Cross. I honor You & I receive the spirit of adoption deep into my heart today (Galatians 4:6). Thank You that I am not rejected. I am adopted, chosen, received, accepted & grafted into Your family. I renounce & rebuke any spirit of rejection or abandonment that has harassed my life. I decree the manifestation of the spirit of adoption over my life. I receive Your grace & choose today to forgive all those who have hurt, rejected or abandoned me. Thank You Jesus that this forgiveness is going deep into the soil of my heart today. I release those who have hurt me & bless them. I ask that the reality of Your unconditional love would be so real in my life that I would release it everywhere I go. I also decree the spirit of adoption over my family, friends, the Arab community in Israel, the Jewish community in Israel & to the ends of the earth! Thank You Lord for the spirit of adoption. I receive it afresh today in Jesus' name.

Day Ten
Church of the Holy Sepulcher

Church of the Holy Sepulcher

Scripture Reading:

"Jesus said to her, 'I am the resurrection and the life. He who believes in me will live, even though he dies; and whoever lives and believes in me will never die. Do you believe this?' 'Yes, Lord,' she told him, 'I believe that you are the Christ, the Son of God, who was to come into the world.'" (John 11:25-27)

About These Photographs:

These are photos from the Holy Church of the Sepulcher, also called the Church of the Resurrection. It is in the Christian Quarter of the Old City. Catholics believe that this was the site of Calvary & also the place where Jesus was buried. It is a very popular pilgrimage site. One of the most striking things about the church is how the light penetrates in from the outside. All through out Basilica are beautiful candles that create an atmosphere for contemplation & prayer.

Decree / Prayer an Increased Measure of Faith: *Lord, I thank You for Your Word which teaches us that without faith it is impossible to please You (Hebrews 11:6). With this in mind, I decree a fresh spirit of faith over my heart, soul & mind today. I declare John 11:27 over myself, "Yes, Lord: I believe You are the Christ, the Son of God." Thank You that You give grace to each person as You have apportioned it (Ephesians 4:7) & that You also said that You would not withhold a good gift from me if I ask (Matthew 11:7). So I ask & receive an increased measure of faith today in Jesus' name. Let the spirit of faith penetrate all that I do & all that I am. I also release a fresh spirit of faith over my loved ones in Jesus' name. Thank You for opening our eyes afresh to know You & Your ways in increasing measure. Finally Lord, I pray for a fresh spirit of faith to come to the streets of Jerusalem today. Reveal Yourself in power to those who do not yet know You in Jerusalem, Israel & to the ends of the earth.*

Day Eleven
Arab Children

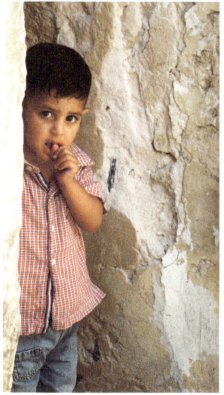
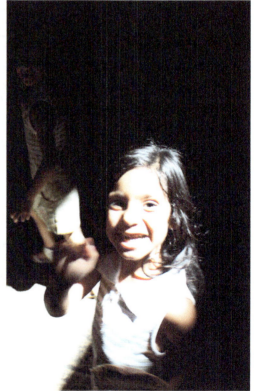

Arab Children

Scripture Reading:

"People were also bringing babies to Jesus to have him touch them. When the disciples saw this, they rebuked them. But Jesus called the children to him and said, 'Let the little children come to me, and do not hinder them, for the kingdom of God belongs to such as these. I tell you the truth, anyone who will not receive the kingdom of God like a little child will never enter it.'"

(Luke 18:15-17)

About These Photographs:

These are pictures of Arab children in the Arab market located in the Old City of Jerusalem. Children are an integral part of every day life in Jerusalem's market. You will see them selling food, hauling supplies or simply running & playing in the streets.

Decree / Prayer for Childlike Hearts & for Children to Come to Jesus: *Jesus, I thank You that You taught us that we should receive the Kingdom of God like a little child (Matthew 18:3). I ask that You would give me a childlike heart to believe & receive all of Your Kingdom truths. If You said it, I choose to believe it. In every area where my heart has become jaded or skeptical towards You or others, I ask for a fresh outpouring of a childlike spirit that brings You pleasure. I also repent for any judgments I have made, bitterness or anger that I have harbored in my heart which would steal my joy or decrease my receptivity to Your truths. Thank You for renewing & expanding a holy childlike nature in me today. I also pray for children everywhere. Jesus, You said to let the little children come to You (Matthew 19:14). I pray that today there would be a great 'coming' of children all over the world to You. I pray for Arab children, for Jewish children & children all over the world. I decree a fresh wave of revelation through dreams, visions & encounters with You. Today, I call in a massive harvest of souls amongst the children of the earth. (If applicable) I also speak a blessing over my current & future lineage. I bless my children to know You powerfully, to have a childlike spirit that pleases Your heart & to make You known. I declare that my natural & spiritual children are set apart to make You famous in the earth. Protect them, fashion them, empower them & seal them into Your perfect will in Jesus' name.*

Day Twelve
The Arab Quarter

The Arab Quarter

Scripture Reading:

"Early the next morning Abraham took some food and a skin of water and gave them to Hagar. He set them on her shoulders and then sent her off with the boy...God heard the boy crying, and the angel of God called to Hagar from heaven... '...Lift the boy up and take him by the hand, for I will make him into a great nation.'" (Genesis 21:14-18)

About These Photographs:

The top photograph here shows a view of one of the streets in the Arab market in the Old City of Jerusalem. It is full of color & opportunities to spend on a variety of market items such as clothing, food, jewelry & a whole lot more. The photograph on the bottom left is of a few Arab men sitting at an entrance which takes walkers deeper into the Arab Quarter & eventually to the Temple Mount. On the bottom right is an Arab man heading towards the Damascus Gate in the wall around the Old City of Jerusalem. There is always lots of hustle & bustle in these areas. It seems the city never sleeps.

Decree / Prayer for the Harvest: *Father, I thank You that You always hear our cry (Psalm 116:1). Just as You heard the cry of Ishmael when he was rejected by Abraham in Genesis 21, You also hear the inner cry of all those who do not yet know You. Lord, today in prayer, I call forth the harvest of the nations. I pray for the Arab nations. Lord, I loose the realm of dreams, visions & encounters that would draw them to the revelation of salvation through Christ. I call forth this same thing for the Jewish people. Reveal the Messiah to them I pray. I also pray for the nations of the earth. Holy Spirit, visit people all over the world today & reveal the mercy of Christ's saving grace & power. Father, I thank You that Your arm is not too short to save & Your light is not too weak to penetrate even the darkest of places (Isaiah 59:1). I pray especially for those in the nations of the earth where terror, abuse, exploitation, violence, perversion or anything that does not honor You is being perpetuated. God, would You break in on their worlds today in Jesus' name. I call forth Saul to Paul encounters all over the world right now in Jesus' name. May those who are persecuting Your ways or Your people encounter You in such a way that they will become the greatest advocates of the Gospel in this generation. I call forth this harvest in Jesus' name. Thank You for hearing this cry.*

Day Thirteen

Jewish Children

Jewish Children

Scripture Reading:

'The city streets will be filled with boys and girls playing there.' This is what the LORD Almighty says: 'It may seem marvelous to the remnant of this people at that time, but will it seem marvelous to me?' declares the LORD Almighty. This is what the LORD Almighty says: 'I will save my people from the countries of the east and the west. I will bring them back to live in Jerusalem; they will be my people, and I will be faithful and righteous to them as their God."
(Zechariah 8:5-8)

About These Photographs:

The streets of the Jewish Quarter of the Old City are full of life. Pick any street during the daytime & you will very likely encounter a group of playing children, women shuffling their families from place to place, Jewish men walking to a synagogue & more. Both the city & the people are beautiful & a modern day picture of the prophecy in Zechariah 8 fulfilled.

Decree / Prayer Giving Thanks For God's Faithfulness To His Promises: *Father, I thank You for Your faithfulness to Your promises. I thank You for Your promises in my life which have already been fulfilled & I decree that every promise You have for me will come to pass in my life. I thank You for the promise of Your provision, that You will never leave me or forsake me, that You are my Healer, my Savior, my Deliverer, Protector & that You will withhold no good thing from me as Your child (Matthew 7:11). I honor You for Your faithfulness. I decree that everything that is resisting the manifestation of Your promises in my life, or the lives of my loved ones, is being removed now in Jesus' name. I resist & rebuke all hindrances or forces in my life contrary to Your perfect will. I also repent for any way that I have repelled Your promises through unbelief, wrong thinking or wrong expectations. I renounce any way that my thought life, emotional life or behavior has blocked the release of Your power & promises. I call forth Your alignment over my life, & the lives of my loved ones, now in Jesus' name. I persist in faith knowing that You are always faithful & Your promises will manifest in my life as I lay hold of them, receive them & do not give up believing. I also thank You for Your promises to the Jewish people that you would send them their Messiah. I ask that the revelation of Your promise fulfilled in Jesus would come to them today in Jesus' name.*

Day Fourteen
Elderly Jewish Men

Elderly Jewish Men

Scripture Reading:

"This is what the LORD says: 'I will return to Zion and dwell in Jerusalem. Then Jerusalem will be called the City of Truth, and the mountain of the LORD Almighty will be called the Holy Mountain.' This is what the LORD Almighty says: 'Once again men and women of ripe old age will sit in the streets of Jerusalem, each with cane in hand because of his age.'"

(Zechariah 8:3-4)

About These Photographs:

All throughout the Old City & the Jewish Quarter you will see the elderly. They are at the Western Wall praying, in the market areas doing business, in the synagogues & walking in the streets. Their presence is a powerful fulfillment of Zechariah 8:3-4.

Prayer / Decree for Longevity & To Release Honour:
Lord, I thank You for the blessing of longevity & for the precious elderly in our generation who have worked in the hopes of of giving us a better future. I honor them before You today & ask that You would strengthen them in body & spirit. I pray for this blessing to be upon the fathers & mothers in my life. Thank You for the promise of Your Word which says if I honor my father & mother then I will live a long life (Exodus 20:12). I lay hold of this admonition to honor, & the blessing of long life, in Jesus' name. I ask that You would shine the light of Your conviction on my heart right now if there is any way that I have not followed Your Word to honor my biological, spiritual, or national fathers & mothers. I repent & ask that You would show me how to make it right. I receive a fresh revelation & empowerment of the spirit of honor today in Jesus' name & thank You for it. I also thank You for Your faithfulness to the nation of Israel. I pray You would bless the elderly in the streets of Jerusalem today. I ask that the revelation of honor would go deep into my heart & that I would walk in it everywhere I go. I also ask that You would empower me to be a father/mother of courage, wisdom, strength, holiness & truth that will help build a better world for future generations. I receive this empowerment by faith right now in Your name & for Your glory.

Day Fifteen
Jewish Families & Children

Jewish Families & Children at the Western Wall

Scripture Reading:

"This is what the Sovereign LORD says: "See, I will beckon to the Gentiles, I will lift up my banner to the peoples; they will bring your sons in their arms and carry your daughters on their shoulders.""
(Isaiah 49:22)

About These Photographs:

In these photographs are a lovely Jewish family, a young boy walking & a group of boys watching soldiers at a check point near the Western Wall. Each photograph is a tangible snapshot of God's answered promise to the Jewish people to bring them back to live in Israel. In these days the Lord is drawing many Jewish people to settle back in the modern nation of Israel. Furthermore, many of them are returning with the help of Christians who have been moved by God to help. The term used to describe the returning of the Jewish people from the nations back to Israel is *aliyah* which, in Hebrew, means *ascent*.

Prayer / Decree Calling Forth Inheritance & Israel's Aliyah: *Father God, we thank You for Your faithfulness to Your promises to natural Israel & to those of us who have been grafted in through Jesus (Romans 11:17). I call forth the full manifestation of my inheritance in You. I call this forth for my life & into the lives of my loved ones as well. I also pray for the natural seed of Israel. I pray that they too would receive their rightful inheritance through You. I ask that You would grant me an increased revelation of Your heart for Israel, Your covenant with them & Your desire for them in this hour of human history. I desire to partner with You in the fullness of Your will. Open my eyes to understand what that is as it relates to the Jewish people. In addition to revelation, grant me grace to be a ready & willing volunteer in the day of Your power (Psalm 110:3). I desire to partner with You in blessing Israel. Open my eyes to ways I can assist those You are drawing to make aliyah. Thank You Jesus for the privilege of partnering with You in Your plan for natural Israel. I offer my hands willingly today. I also call forth the revelation of Your heart for Israel into my nation, the Arab nations & all the nations of the earth. Father, give us Your heart for the Jewish people in the name of Yeshua (Jesus).*

Day Sixteen
The City of David

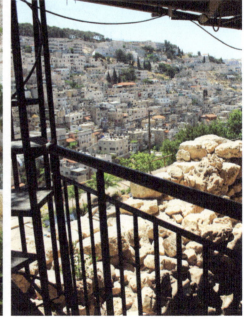

The City of David

Scripture Reading:

"Of the increase of his government and peace there will be no end. He will reign on David's throne and over his kingdom, establishing and upholding it with justice and righteousness from that time on and forever. The zeal of the LORD Almighty will accomplish this…Then Jesus came to them and said, 'All authority in heaven and on earth has been given to me…'"
(Isaiah 9:7 & Matthew 28:18)

About These Photographs:

These photographs are from the City of David. It is just outside the Old City of Jerusalem on a ridge that runs from the Temple Mount. Not only is the City of David the oldest settled area of Jerusalem & therefore a major archeological dig site (see dig picture on the bottom right side), but it is also the place where King David built his palace in Jerusalem & established his capitol. Today it is full of homes belonging to both Jewish & Arab families, some who have archeological digs happening all around their homes.

Prayer / Decree for God's Rule Through His People (Authority): *Lord, I thank You for Your rulership, dominion & authority. I declare You are King & Lord over my life. I release Your dominion over my family & loved ones today. In addition I call all things in my life & theirs into alignment with Your righteousness. Jesus, thank You that You have authority over death & that You have released that authority to Your people (Matthew 28:18-19). I take these keys of authority by faith in Jesus' name. I receive fresh understanding & wisdom to know how to use them to bind the works of the enemy & loose heaven on earth (Matthew 18:18). Use me to liberate the oppressed, heal the sick & bring Your resurrection power into situations around me. I also pray for a fresh release of Your rulership & dominion to be manifested through Your people in Jerusalem, Israel & to the ends of the earth. I call forth a people who will arise, shine & push back the works of darkness in Jesus' name. I thank You Jesus that of the increase of Your government there will be no diminishing (Isaiah 9:7) & I step into reality of this today. I give You my life. Use me to advance Your rule in the earth, I pray.*

Day Seventeen

Jewish Tombs

The Jewish Tombs

Scripture Reading:

"And when Jesus had cried out again in a loud voice, he gave up his spirit. At that moment the curtain of the temple was torn in two from top to bottom. The earth shook and the rocks split. The tombs broke open and the bodies of many holy people who had died were raised to life. They came out of the tombs, and after Jesus' resurrection they went into the holy city and appeared to many people." (Matthew 27:50-53) "Listen, I tell you a mystery: We will not all sleep, but we will all be changed-- in a flash, in the twinkling of an eye, at the last trumpet. For the trumpet will sound, the dead will be raised imperishable, and we will be changed." (1 Corinthians 15:51-52)

About These Photographs:

This is the Jewish grave site on the Mount of Olives. It is directly across from the Eastern Wall of the Old City of Jerusalem. A Jewish custom of honor is to place small stones on top of the graves, like in the photograph on the top left. Jewish graves fill the mountainside & stairwells & cascade down the mountain so that visitors can make their way between the row upon row of graves.

Prayer / Decree Asking for an Eternal Mindset: *Holy Spirit, I thank You for giving me a revelation of eternity. I believe Your Word which says we will live forever & that time is finite (Matthew 24:35). Today, I decree a fresh revelation of eternity into my heart, soul & mind in Jesus' name. I choose to live in light of eternity & ask that You would give me the grace to see every situation through the lens of eternity. I recognize that Your Word clearly teaches that every word I speak & deed I do will be tested on the Day of Judgment & that only the things I do out of a pure motive will remain (1 Corinthians 3:12). Today, I call forth the fire of Your purity to refine my motives & empower me to build my life in a way that will lead to treasure in eternity, not only treasure on earth. Help me to understand, with increasing wisdom, what this means practically in my day to day life. I turn away from carnal living & choose to store up treasure in heaven where moth & rust cannot destroy (Matthew 6:20). Jesus, thank You for Your saving grace & that I will live with You forever in heaven because of Your sacrifice on the Cross. I also loose this revelation of eternity into the hearts of my loved ones, the inhabitants of Jerusalem, Israel & those in the nations of the earth. Thank You for the revelation of eternity that You are putting in our hearts.*

Day Eighteen

Israeli Defense Force

Israel Defense Forces

Scripture Reading:

"I have posted watchmen on your walls, O Jerusalem; they will never be silent day or night. You who call on the LORD, give yourselves no rest, and give him no rest till he establishes Jerusalem and makes her the praise of the earth." (Isaiah 62: 6–7)

About These Photographs:

Though for the most part, Israel is a very peaceful place the Israeli Defense Forces (IDF) are ready for potential acts of war against Israel at any moment & work daily to secure Israel's borders. The top photograph is of an IDF vehicle patrolling in the desert. The photograph at the bottom left shows barb wire fencing that laces the tops of many walls throughout the Jewish Quarter in the Old City of Jerusalem. The photograph at the bottom right is of an underground army bunker in northern Israel.

Prayer / Decree for Protection: *Lord, thank You that Your Word says You watch over Israel & You never sleep nor slumber (Psalm 121:4). In the same way I thank You that You watch over my life continuously. I decree the manifestation of Your protection over my life & the lives of my loved ones today in Jesus' name. I thank You that no weapon formed against me will prosper & that every tongue that rises up in accusation against me is cast down in Jesus' name (Isaiah 54:17). I decree Your protection & victory over my health, emotions, relationships, finances, future & family. I call back anything that the enemy has stolen, with seven fold interest, in Jesus' name (Proverbs 6:31). Thank You also for the peace of Jerusalem & Israel. I decree a release of Your Spirit on all those who have hatred in their hearts towards Israel. Lead them to Jesus & cause the spirit of reconciliation to fill their hearts, I pray. I speak a blessing over the IDF today in Jesus' name. Holy Spirit, I ask that You would draw IDF soldiers to the saving knowledge of the Messiah, Jesus Christ. Renew them in purity & equip them to be effective defenders of Israel. I also pray for intercessors globally who have been set apart as spiritual watchmen for our times. Alert them & all who know You to prayer at the right time & in the right ways. Today, I receive a renewed grace to be a spiritual watchman. Thank You that You are alerting me to the schemes of the enemy against my life & my loved ones & equipping me to swiftly cut them off. Thank You for Your divine protection. I decree it now in Jesus' name.*

Day Nineteen

The Security Wall

The Security Wall

Scripture Reading:

"But now in Christ Jesus you who once were far away have been brought near through the blood of Christ. For he himself is our peace, who has made the two one and has destroyed the barrier, the dividing wall of hostility, by abolishing in his flesh the law with its commandments and regulations. His purpose was to create in himself one new man out of the two, thus making peace, and in this one body to reconcile both of them to God through the cross, by which he put to death their hostility." (Ephesians 2:13-16)

About These Photographs:

These photographs are of the security wall in Israel which divides Jerusalem & Bethlehem. It runs continuously for several hundred kilometers between Israel & the Palestinian West Bank. Artisitic graffeti on it reflects a longing for peace & reconciliation.

Prayer / Decree For the Spirit of Reconciliation: *Jesus, I thank You that You are the Prince of Peace & the only source of lasting peace. I pray that Your shalom (peace) would fill the hearts of Arabs, Jews & all those who are struggling with relational strife. I decree & call forth Your shalom to come to Israel today & all nations experiencing war. I also decree Your peace into my life. I receive Your shalom today & call forth an increased measure of the fruit of peace in my life. I thank You that You have called us to be ambassadors of Your reconciliation & I receive fresh empowerment today to be one who brings Your peace wherever I go (2 Corinthians 5:20). I speak to every one of my relationships & over my loved ones & declare that Your peace would fill our hearts & lives today. May all our relationships enjoy an increased level of harmony & shalom. Where strife has prevailed in my heart, or the hearts of my loved ones, I call forth healing & reconciliation in Jesus' name. Where unforgiveness has prevailed I decree a supernatural ability to forgive & love those who have hurt us. Father, I ask for a wave of Your peace to come to my life, my loved ones' lives, the Jewish community, the Arab community & to the ends of the earth today in Jesus' name.*

Day Twenty

The Dead Sea

The Dead Sea

Scripture Reading:

"You are the salt of the earth. But if the salt loses its saltiness, how can it be made salty again? It is no longer good for anything, except to be thrown out and trampled by men." (Matthew 5:13)

About These Photographs:

This is the Dead Sea, also known as the Salt Sea. The eastern side of the Dead Sea belongs to the Jordan & the western side to Israel. The white substance covering the rocks & ground in these photographs is salt. When it comes to the Dead Sea, salt is everywhere. It is both in the water & on the shores. A popular tourist activity in Israel traveling to the Dead Sea for a 'bob' (as opposed to a swim).

Prayer / Decree to be the Salt of the Earth: *Jesus, I thank You that You said that as Your followers we are the salt of the earth. We are called to bring preservation & holy flavor to the world around us. Today, I decree & receive a fresh empowerment upon my life to manifest this kind of saltiness for Your glory. I ask that You would transform me & fill me with Your Spirit afresh so that I might display, advance & create Your righteousness wherever I go. I call forth Your righteousness & Your justice into my life, the lives of my loved ones, my nation & the nations of the earth. I pray You would fill the earth with Your righteousness Lord & use my life to help do it. I also call forth Your empowering grace upon believers everywhere. I pray that Your Church worldwide would manifest Your righteousness in an awesome way that reveals Christ & draws multitudes to You. I decree that every area in my life, my loved ones, my nation & the nations of the earth that does not reflect Your righteousness is being shaken now in Jesus' name. Replace any of these areas with Your character I pray. Thank You Jesus for Your righteousness.*

Day Twenty-One
Masada

Masada

Scripture Reading:

"The LORD thunders at the head of his army; his forces are beyond number, and mighty are those who obey his command. The day of the LORD is great; it is dreadful. Who can endure it? 'Even now," declares the LORD, "return to me with all your heart…'"
(Joel 2:11-12a)

About These Photographs:

These photographs are of the famous fortress known as Masada. It is located on the top of a massive rock plateau overlooking the Dead Sea in the dessert of Israel. The fortress was built by Herod the Great as a refuge. It was taken captive in 66 AD by a Jewish group rebelling against the Roman Empire. Eventually the Romans laid siege to Masada. They built a massive ramp & after some time, the Roman soldiers finally reached the top. When they arrived they found a surprise. In an act of determination not to be taken captive, the Jewish community had committed mass suicide. Because of this, Masada is viewed by many in Israel as a symbol of national resolve. The Israeli Defense Forces (IDF) have a practice of holding their graduation ceremony for soldiers at Masada.

Prayer / Decree for Perseverance and Determination: *Today, I call forth & decree a fresh spirit of determination & perseverance over my life & the lives of my loved ones. I thank You Lord that Your Word promises that if we do not grow weary in doing good we will reap a reward, if we do not give up (Galatians 6:9). I repent for times when I have not persevered in doing what is right. Today, I determine afresh not to give up in doing good, even when I don't feel like it or when I don't see results right away. I also call forth & decree this same spirit of determination & perseverance over my loved ones. Thank You for giving us the grace to run the distance when it comes to living a Godly life that honors You. Last of all, I decree the spirit of determination & perseverance in doing what is right to come to the leaders of my nation, the cultural leaders of our time, justice activists, the leaders of Israel & global leaders. God, grant them grace to stand for righteousness, justice & to be a voice on behalf of the poor, oppressed & voiceless no matter what the cost. Thank You Lord, for making me a person of perseverance by Your empowering grace. I receive it today in Jesus' name.*

Day Twenty-Two

Desert Caves

Qumran Desert Caves

Scripture Reading:

"A voice of one calling: 'In the desert prepare the way for the LORD; make straight in the wilderness a highway for our God. Every valley shall be raised up, every mountain and hill made low; the rough ground shall become level, the rugged places a plain. And the glory of the LORD will be revealed, and all mankind together will see it. For the mouth of the LORD has spoken.'" (Isaiah 40:3-5)

About These Photographs:

These photographs were taken at Qumran, the site in the West Bank where the Dead Sea Scrolls were discovered in the 1940s. At Qumran archeologists have found caves, Jewish settlements, ritual baths & cemeteries. Many believe the location was likely home to the Jewish sect called the Essenes who were known for abstaining from worldly pleasures & who devoted their lives to studying the Torah. Some believe John the Baptist spent time in these communities.

Prayer / Decree to Discover God's Hidden Treasures:
Lord, thank You that You said You will reward all those who diligently seek You (Hebrews 11:6). I set my heart to diligently seek You afresh today. I decree a new hunger in my soul to learn more about Your Word, Your heart & Your ways. I decree & call forth fresh revelation of Your truth into my mind. As I read Your Word, I declare that I will understand Biblical truths & see things in Your Word that I have never seen or understood before. I desire to comprehend Your mysteries Lord. I ask for an increase in the gifts of discernment, wisdom, knowledge & prophecy in my life & in the lives of my loved ones (1 Corinthians 12:8-10). I thank You that we are growing in these gifts daily for Your glory. I also call forth an increase of dreams & visions into my life that will draw me closer to You & reveal Your ways to me (Joel 2:28-29). I ask that You would reveal to me anything in my life that is hindering my growth in You. As You reveal these hidden things, I receive the grace to deal with them & rid my life of them. I also call forth deeper understanding of Your heart for me, Your thoughts towards me & Your will for my life. I ask for understanding of the things that have been hidden from me. You said that You desire truth in my inner parts & I desire this as well (Psalm 51:6). I thank You for granting me wisdom & revelation today to discover Your truths. I call these same things forward for my loved ones as well. Thank You Jesus.

Day Twenty-Three
The Bedouins

The Bedouin People

Scripture Reading:

"The LORD had said to Abram, 'Leave your country, your people and your father's household and go to the land I will show you. 'I will make you into a great nation and I will bless you; I will make your name great, and you will be a blessing....'"
(Genesis 12:1-2)

About These Photographs:

The Israelis in these photographys are known as Bedouins. They are desert-dwelling people who sleep in tents & are often found herding sheep in the countryside. Some are known to keep camels like the one in the top picture. If you are blessed to meet one who has a camel you have the opportunity for a ride.

Prayer / Decree to Be Led By God's Voice: *Lord, I thank You that Your Word says that Your sheep hear Your voice & that they will not follow the voice of another (John 10:5). I thank You that because I have given my life to You I am one of Your sheep (John 10:27). Therefore, I will hear Your voice. In addition, I decree & call forth an increased ability to not only hear Your voice but to recognize it. I decree this both for myself & my loved ones in Jesus' name. I thank You that when I recognize Your voice I will also understand what You are communicating without distortion. I rebuke the spirit of confusion & decree accurate hearing over my life in Jesus' name. I also thank You that I am not only a hearer of Your Word but a doer also (James 1:22). I hear Your voice & I follow You no matter where You are leading. Just as Abram followed Your voice as You led him to the land of Israel, so I declare over my life that I will follow Your voice wherever You lead. Thank You that I have clear understanding of Your will as well as the grace & courage to do whatever You say. I receive this afresh today. I also pray for all of my loved ones & any of Your children who are struggling with hearing Your voice & following. May Your clarity & courage come to them today in Jesus' name. Thank You for Your voice which faithfully leads us Lord.*

Day Twenty-Four
Capernaum

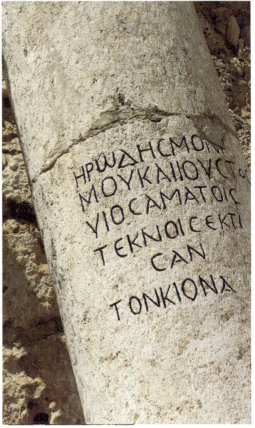

Capernaum

Scripture Reading:

"They went to Capernaum, and when the Sabbath came, Jesus went into the synagogue and began to teach. The people were amazed at his teaching, because he taught them as one who had authority, not as the teachers of the law. Just then a man in their synagogue who was possessed by an evil spirit... 'Be quiet!' said Jesus sternly. 'Come out of him!' The evil spirit shook the man violently and came out of him with a shriek. The people were all so amazed that they asked each other, 'What is this? A new teaching--and with authority! He even gives orders to evil spirits and they obey him.'" (Mark1:21-27)

About These Photographs:

The top photograph is of the synagogue in Capernaum where the story in Mark 1 took place. Capernaum was Jesus' home base during His earthly ministry. The photgraph at the bottom right is of one of the synagogue pillars. The photograph on the bottom left shows the remains of buildings (likely Jewish homes) surrounding the synagogue. Capernaum is a humble village just up a hill on the northern shore of the Sea of Galilee.

Prayer / Decree for Signs & Wonders Confirming that Jesus is Messiah: *Jesus, I thank You that when You preached, You did it with authority. The miracles You performed & the authority You demonstrated confirmed that You are the Messiah. I also thank You that You said if I believed, I would do even greater works than this (John 14:12-14). I choose to believe Your Word & I call forth a greater manifestation of Your authority & miracle working power through my life. Let it demonstrate that You are the Savior of the world! I also decree an increased level of faith into my heart & Your church at large to step out & work miracles in a way that will compel skeptics to turn to You. I call forth a fresh boldness to cast out demons, heal the sick & raise the dead. I thank You Lord that You are the same yesterday, today & forever (Hebrews 13:8). I call forth daily divine appointments for my life. I ask for opportunities to step out & display Your power daily for Your glory. When these opportunities come, I thank You that I will recognize them & have the boldness to step out. I will not shrink back but will stretch forth my hand to a hurting world with Your love & power in Jesus' name. If I step out & nothing seems to happen, I will keep stepping out. I will not shrink back. Jesus, thank You for displaying Your power, for Your glory, through my life in Jesus' name.*

Day Twenty-Five
The Galilee

The Sea of Galilee

Scripture Reading:

"Leaving Nazareth, he went and lived in Capernaum, which was by the lake in the area of Zebulun and Naphtali-- to fulfill what was said through the prophet Isaiah: 'Land of Zebulun and land of Naphtali, the way to the sea, along the Jordan, Galilee of the Gentiles - the people living in darkness have seen a great light; on those living in the land of the shadow of death a light has dawned.' From that time on Jesus began to preach, 'Repent, for the kingdom of heaven is near.'"
(Matthew 4:13-17)

About These Photographs:

These are photos of the stunning Sea of Galilee. Much of Jesus' earthly ministry took place around the Sea of Galilee. This is where both Jesus & Peter walked on water. It is also where Simon Peter & Andrew were fishing when Jesus found them & called them to leave their fishing trade in order to be His disciples.

Prayer / Decree to Shine the Light of Jesus' Presence:
Thank You Lord that You told us to let our light shine before men so that people would see our good works & praise our Father in Heaven. I desire to shine for You wherever I go & to anyone I meet. Holy Spirit, I call forth an increased manifestation of Your fruit in my life to enable me to shine the character of Christ. I decree & call forth an increased measure of Your love, joy, peace, patience, kindness, goodness, faithfulness, gentleness & self-control to be manifested in & through my life (Galatians 5:22-23). I especially call forth an increase of the fruit of love in my life. I decree that I am growing in love for You & those around me every day. I ask that You would show me any areas in my heart where lack of love resides. If there is any bitterness, judgment, strife, pride, anger, hatred, or the like I give You permission to expose & uproot it in Jesus' name. I turn away from spiritual darkness in all its forms, I renounce it & I turn to You Lord. Holy Spirit, fill me with the light of Your presence so that the world will see & be drawn to salvation through Christ. I also pray for my family, friends, the Jewish people & all the gentile nations – I call forth the manifestation of Your light & truth into all our midst. Draw us all to Your light in a powerful way today, I pray in Jesus' name.

Day Twenty-Six
Mount of Beatitudes

The Mount of Beatitudes

Scripture Reading:

"...and he began to teach them, saying: 'Blessed are the poor in spirit, for theirs is the kingdom of heaven. Blessed are those who mourn, for they will be comforted. Blessed are the meek, for they will inherit the earth. Blessed are those who hunger and thirst for righteousness, for they will be filled. Blessed are the merciful, for they will be shown mercy. Blessed are the pure in heart, for they will see God. Blessed are the peacemakers, for they will be called sons of God. Blessed are those who are persecuted because of righteousness, for theirs is the kingdom of heaven.'"

(Matthew 5:2-10)

About These Photographs:

This is the Basilica on the Mount of Beatitudes. This is the location where it is believed Jesus delivered *The Sermon on the Mount* in Matthew 5. The nun in the photograph on the bottom left has been greeting visitors to the Mount for years. The location is gorgeous as it overlooks the Sea of Galilee & the hills surrounding.

Prayer / Decree to Live the Sermon on the Mount Lifestyle: *Jesus, I embrace Your teachings with my whole heart. I decree over my heart, soul & mind the attributes You esteemed in Matthew 5:1-10. I decree over my life the ability to be poor in spirit. I want to hunger for You in increased measure. I receive the grace to mourn in a health way. I declare that I will be healed of past losses & move forward into the fullness of Your comfort. I decree a spirit of meekness over my soul & call forth Your promise that I will inherit the earth as I walk in that meekness. I decree a fresh hunger & thirst for Your righteousness over my soul. I thank You that as I hunger & thirst for righteousness I will be filled. I decree a spirit of purity into my heart. Please remove anything that does not reflect Your holiness. I desire to see God. I decree a supernatural ability over my life to be a peacemaker. Lord, make me a mature child of God. I also thank You for the times & ways that I experience persecution for Your name's sake. Thank You that You promised if I was persecuted for righteousness sake, I would have a great reward in heaven. Father, I call forth all these things into my life & the lives of my loved ones. I also pray that Your people across the world would walk in Your exhortation to meekness, forgiveness & that we would bless those who curse us. Thank You that as we do this we will be a powerful wittness of Your love & reality to those who do not yet know You (Matthew 5:16). Holy Spirit, work in me to make me more like Jesus, I pray.*

Day Twenty-Seven

Gideon's Brook

Gideon's Brooks

Scripture Reading:

"…the LORD said to Gideon, 'There are still too many men. Take them down to the water, and I will sift them for you there…' So Gideon took the men down to the water. There the LORD told him, 'Separate those who lap the water with their tongues like a dog from those who kneel down to drink.' Three hundred men lapped with their hands to their mouths. All the rest got down on their knees to drink. The LORD said to Gideon, 'With the three hundred men that lapped I will save you and give the Midianites into your hands.'"

(Judges 7:4-7)

About These Photographs:

This is the river where it is believed Gideon & his men drank in Judges 7. The river is in a lush valley surrounded by large trees. Today the water is clear, beautiful & easy to drink just as it was in Gideon's time.

Prayer / Decree to Trust God in the Midst Of Battles: *God, I thank You that You are God & I am not. I choose today to put my faith in Your strength alone. As I face life's battles I trust in Your ability instead of my own power. I thank You that in my weakness Your strength is made perfect (2 Corinthians 12:9). Like Gideon, I make a conscious choice to do things Your way instead of what makes sense to my natural mind or the world's system. I also ask that You would reveal to me any way that I am not trusting in You so that I can adjust. I declare that I will make any needed adjustments swiftly. I also decree a fresh measure of faith into my life & the lives of my loved ones. I declare that we will trust You in the midst of life's challenges. I speak to every battle, ungodly obstacle & hindrance in my life & the lives of my loved ones & I call forth Your supernatural intervention in Jesus' mighty name. I also call forth angelic assistance & thank You for it. I realize that my battle is not against flesh & blood & so I lift up my shield of faith right now (Ephesians 6:12-16). I thank You that Your Word says this shield will extinguish every one of the enemy's firey darts. I fix my eyes on You & Your power. I put my hand in Yours & walk forward in trust. I thank Y that sickness, strife, poverty & every disorder that has come against me or my loved ones is fleeing now in Jesus' name. I decree that Your will & the victory of the Cross is prevailing over our lives today & will prevail for all our days. I decree over my life, & the lives of my loved ones, that You win!*

Day Twenty-Eight
Joppa

Joppa

Scripture Reading:

"In Joppa there was a disciple named Tabitha (which, when translated, is Dorcas), who was always doing good and helping the poor. About that time she became sick and died...Lydda was near Joppa; so when the disciples heard that Peter was in Lydda, they sent two men to him and urged him, 'Please come at once!' Peter went with them, and when he arrived he was taken upstairs to the room...Turning toward the dead woman, he said, 'Tabitha, get up.' She opened her eyes, and seeing Peter she sat up." (Acts 9:36-40)

About These Photographs:

These photographs are taken of modern day Joppa, the location of Tabitha's resurrection. Peter stayed in Joppa for a season. It is the place where, one morning during prayer, the Lord commissioned Peter through a trance to preach the Gospel to the gentiles. His first assignment to do this happened just moments later when he was called to visit Cornelius in Caesarea.

Prayer / Decree for a Rising of Those Who Will Advance Mercy & Justice: *Father, I thank You for the powerful example of Tabitha's life & how she displays Your call to advance mercy & justice in the earth. I acknowlege that Your Word exhorts me to do justice, to love mercy & to walk humbly before You (Micah 6:8). I decree over my life, & the lives of my loved ones, that we are growing in good works & charitable deeds daily. I speak to my spiritual eyes & call forth an increased ability to see the needs around me. As I see them, I declare that I will respond with Your love, kindness & in any way You empower me. Fill my life, I pray, so that I can be a blessing to those around me. I also speak to my ears to be able to hear Your voice regarding the needs You want me to meet - whether right in front of me or on the other side of the world. I desire to partner with You to touch the needs of those around me. Furthermore, I ask that You would increase this desire in my heart more & more each day. As Tabitha arose, I declare that I too will rise & do works of righteousness & justice. I also pray for Your Church at large. I call forth an increased measure of love & empowerment for us all to do deeds of love & advance Your goodness through our lives. I call forth Your favor on Your Church to be positioned among governments & rulers in the earth to be the answer to our generation's needs. Father, let Your Church arise & shine Your mercy, goodness, love & power to the earth like no generation has ever seen!*

Day Twenty-Nine
Caesarea

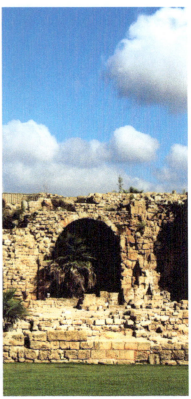

Caesara

Scripture Reading:

"The following day [Peter] arrived in Caesarea. Cornelius was expecting them...[Peter said], May I ask why you sent for me?' Cornelius answered: 'Four days ago I was in my house praying at this hour, at three in the afternoon. Suddenly a man in shining clothes stood before me and said, 'Cornelius, God has heard your prayer and remembered your gifts to the poor. Send to Joppa for Simon who is called Peter. He is a guest in the home of Simon the tanner, who lives by the sea.' So I sent for you immediately...Then Peter began to speak: 'I now realize how true it is that God does not show favoritism...'" (Acts 10:24-34)

About These Photographs:

This is Caesarea. It was build by Herod the Great & over the centuries was occupied by the Roman Empire, the Byzantines & Arabs. Today the population is around 5,000 & is a very popular tourist stop because of the beautiful historical ruins. Many refer to it as the Palm Springs of Israel. Caesarea is the location Peter was sent to when commissioned by the Lord to go & pray for the gentile named Cornelius.

Prayer / Decree for The Advancement of the Gospel in the Nations: *Jesus, I thank You that You are no respector of persons (Acts 10:34). When You died on the Cross You died for Jews & gentiles alike. Your salvation is for the whole world! I thank You for this powerful reminder through the story of Cornelius. I ask that like You sent Peter to Cornelius, You would send me to those who are ready to receive Your truth. I ask that You would empower me to minister Your love, Your gospel & the Baptism of the Holy Spirit just as Peter did in Acts 10. I receive a fresh commission to 'go' today. I also decree the gifts of discernment, wisdom & knowledge into my life as I reach out in Your name (1 Corinthians 12). I thank You that I will know where to be & when. Today, I call forth an increased ability to connect with people where they are at & draw them deeper into Your arms through Your empowering grace. I also pray for the Church at large. I thank You that we walk in Your love & therefore preach the gospel to the Jewish community, the Arab community & all the gentile nations. I call forth workers to be thrust into the harvest fields of the earth - send them forth today, I pray in Jesus' name. I call forth a massive harvest of souls in our generation for Your glory! Father, in accordance with Your Word, I ask for the nations (Psalm 2:8).*

Day Thirty
Megiddo

Megiddo

Scripture Reading:

"'Behold, I come like a thief! Blessed is he who stays awake and keeps his clothes with him, so that he may not go naked and be shamefully exposed.' Then they gathered the kings together to the place that in Hebrew is called Armageddon. The seventh angel poured out his bowl into the air, and out of the temple came a loud voice from the throne, saying, 'It is done!'"
(Revelation 16:15-17)

About These Photographs:

This is the Valley of Megiddo, called Armageddon in the Book of Revelation. It is the place of the great end time battle that is prophesied in the Book of Revelation. It is situated in close proximity to Mount Carmel, the Jezreel Valley & the brook of Kishon where Elijah slaughtered the prophets of Baal. In contemporary Israel it is a short distance from the modern city of Haifa.

Prayer / Decree to Discern the Times & for the Spirit of Awakening: *Jesus, I thank You that You told us in Your Word that You are coming soon. I believe what You say. Today, I decree the spirit of awakening & alertness over myself. I thank You that I have the anointing to discern the times & to know what to do (1 Chron. 12:32). Thank You that, like the wise virgins, I am alert & awake as I wait for Your return (Matthew 25:1-13). I also decree this over the lives of my loved ones - both those who know You & those who do not yet know You. I declare that I am not moved by any voice other than Yours (John 10:5). I listen for Your voice in the midst of the voices of our generation & put my faith in You alone. Today, I declare that no matter what happens in the world You are able to keep me strong & steady. Jesus, You said in Your Word that nation will rise against nation (Mark 13:8) & everything that can be shaken, will be (Hebrews 12:27). I also call forth a fresh grace for prevailing prayer into my life. When I see shakings in the earth, I declare that I will respond in intercession & faith, not in fear or in murmuring. Thank You Jesus for Your awesome power & victory. There is no force or army in the earth that can stand against You. I decree that my eyes & the eyes of my loved ones are firmly fixed on You & Your Kingdom as we wait to meet You face to face. We love You Jesus. The Spirit & the bride say come (Revelation 22:17).*

Day Thirty-One
Modern Israel

Modern Israel

Scripture Reading:

"Your people will rebuild the ancient ruins and will raise up the age-old foundations; you will be called Repairer of Broken Walls, Restorer of Streets with Dwellings. 'If you keep your feet from breaking the Sabbath and from doing as you please on my holy day, if you call the Sabbath a delight and the LORD's holy day honorable, and if you honor it by not going your own way and not doing as you please or speaking idle words, then you will find your joy in the LORD, and I will cause you to ride on the heights of the land and to feast on the inheritance of your father Jacob.' The mouth of the LORD has spoken." (Isaiah 58:12-14)

About These Photographs:

These photographs are of modern Israel. In them you see Israel rebuilt - a tangible picture of the prophecy of Isaiah 58:12-14 fullfilled in our time. The top photograph & the bottom left photograph are buildings in Tel Aviv at dusk. The building in the bottom right is in the heart of the downtown core of modern Jerusalem. Flowers cascade from every window in a seemingly symbolic statement of new life.

Prayer / Decree for Restoration & New Life: *Jesus, we thank You that You are a restorer & You have the power to make all things new (Rev. 21:5). I honor You for Your restoration power. I decree & call forth a fresh wave of that restoration power into my life & the lives of my loved ones today in Jesus' name. I speak to every area of my life that is in need of a fresh touch of Your restoration power & decree Your power into each of these areas in Jesus' name. Father, I also thank You for Your intent to restore Israel to Yourself through their Messiah Jesus Christ (Yeshua). I recognize that these are the most important 'walls' You desire to rebuild in their midst. I therefore call upon You, Holy Spirit to visit Israel afresh today & draw the Jewish people to the saving knowledge of Yeshua. I call this forth for the Arab people as well. Father, let the restoration that only comes through Jesus invade my life, the lives of my loved ones, the Jewish people of Israel, the Arab nations & all the nations of the earth in Your mighty name! Thank You for Your healing & restoring power. I thank You for how Your restorative power has worked in days past & I thank You in advance for the answers to these prayer & decrees in the days to come. Father, loose Your restoration power in our time like no generation has ever seen.*

About the Author:

Faytene gave her life to Jesus in 1995 & has been a missionary since 1997. In 2011 she married Robert John Grasseschi & they currently serve several non-profit initiatives across North America.

Faytene founded & gives leadership to the MY Canada Association which works to combat various social justice issues such as human trafficking, gendercide, & premature death from natural conception to natural termination. She also serves as the international director of TheCRY Movement, is a best selling author, artist/photographer and seasoned conference speaker.

To find out more about Faytene & Robert's work please visit www.robertjohnandfaytene.com.

Other Resources By Faytene & Robert:

Signature Songs of Extreme Intimacy is a worship CD of songs Faytene wrote & produced in her early years of ministry. *Signature* is full of poems & songs of adoration to Jesus. Many have testified that it is one of their favorite intimacy worship CDs.

Marked: A Generation of Dread Champions Rising To Shift Nations is the story of Faytene & her team's journey of contending to see the nation of Canada impacted for Christ. It is packed full of inspiring stories & powerful principles for anyone wanting to see their nation or sphere influenced for the glory of Jesus Christ.

Stand on Guard: A Prophetic Call & Research on the Righteous Foundations of Canada is Faytene's first book & a national bestseller in Canada. It is 270 pages of research on Canada's Christian heritage & is prefaced by a motivating call to the current generation to arise & reclaim Canada's righteous heritage.

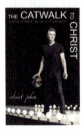

The Catwalk to Christ is the story of Robert John Grasseschi's journey into the loving arms of his heavenly Father from a life filled with heartbreak, trail & pain on the basketball court & in the modeling industry. *The Catwalk to Christ* is a powerful testimony of Father God's love.

Various Art Pieces:

To order these resources visit www.faytene.com.